"*Joy in a Woolly Coat* . . . [is] a very personal, autobiographical account of . . . experiences and relationships with companion animals . . . [it] will bring comfort to those who read the book and are grieving over the loss of beloved companion animals."

> James M. Harris, D.V.M.
> National Authority on Companion Animal Loss
> Montclair Veterinary Clinic and Hospital,
> Oakland, CA

". . . *Joy in a Woolly Coat* . . . addresses the issue of pet loss from a totally new perspective. Thank you for sharing your emotions and discoveries with us."

> Jane Hutchison
> Director of Communications,
> Santa Clara County Humane Society

"Based on her experiences with her pet's deaths and her accompanying feelings of grief, the author sensitively describes those feelings which a pet owner may experience when a beloved companion animal dies."

> Betty J. Carmack, R.N., Ed.D.
> Grief Counselor

"A must for pet lovers . . . *Joy in a Woolly Coat* . . . is a personal account of the strong bonds between pets and their owners . . . poetic in its imagery and emotions . . . [a] simple yet moving story of love."

> Jack Russell
> *San Mateo Times*

Joy in a
Woolly Coat

Joy in a Woolly Coat

*Living with, Loving,
and Letting Go
of Treasured Animal Friends*

JULIE ADAMS CHURCH
Illustrated by CONSTANCE COLEMAN

H J Kramer Inc
Tiburon, California

Published by H J Kramer Inc
P.O. Box 1082, Tiburon, CA 94920

ISBN: 0-915811-08-1

Editing: Kim Peterson
Design and Production: Merrill Peterson
Typesetting: Harrington-Young
Cover Design: Jon Tedesco

Printed in the United States of America

10 9 8 7 6 5 4 3 2 1

Dedicated to
Dietrich Kroger, D.V.M.

Contents

Acknowledgements

Special thanks to Mary R. Stephan who provided continual personal support and a word processor, which made it possible for me to share my thoughts in book form.

For their interest, advice, and support: my sister, Meredith C. Rousseau; my cousin, Catherine McCaffery; and my friend Pamela C. Krawiec.

For the countless hours she spent beautifully designing and coordinating my first edition: Marian O'Brien.

For believing in my message and magnificently capturing the essence of my animal friends: Constance Coleman.

For poem design, "Lady": Juli Crystal.

For her sensitive editing: Kimberley Peterson.

And finally, for their trust and love: Hal and Linda Kramer.

Liberated Lady

Prologue

Lady—what a joy! A new awareness transformed my experience of her death: Lady's essence lived. Her lovely qualities—loyalty, trust, unconditional love—remained even though she had passed out of form. These traits enriched my life and I know that as I contemplate their value I still partake in the life of Lady.

I miss her. I miss her soft white fur and gentle nature. I miss her waiting patiently at my bedside each morning, watching for even the slightest indication of my joining the waking world. For Lady, a mere flutter of my eyelids signaled the dawn of a new day. With unrestrained affection she nuzzled me "good morning," Lady-style, forepaws on the bed, nose buried in the crook of my neck, tail beating rhythmic time on an unseen clock. I miss her woolly presence positioned in passageways and doorways, inviting immediate attention. With tenderness I recall my sweet, dependent, snuggling friend whose keen perceptions belied her inability to hear. She lived her thirteen years in an individual manner with endearing enthusiasm. In one sense those years are over.

Yet in my heart Lady lives. She herself taught me that a life once lived lives forever in the heart.

My experience with this sensitive and devoted dog-lady underscored my quest to learn about the spirit within animals. The questions and answers her death evoked departed considerably from the ideas I had supported most of my life. Until her death, I thought human beings alone possessed an eternal soul. In my view, animals had no soul and were therefore temporal. I now believe that the strong and singular life force which flows through both humans and animals is Spirit—the immortal Spirit that binds all forms of life.

I feel Lady's spirit every day. The best part of her, the part that gave both her life and mine meaning, remains with me still. As with all of life's bonds, the spiritual connection underscores and outlasts the physical relationship.

If we hold this thought as we reflect on the death of an animal companion, perhaps we will find it easier to view its passing with understanding and know some comfort. To our pet, who on earth displayed love and joy and those other qualities that attracted us, going to "the other side" may simply allow that spirit to take off in unbounded happiness, a joyous spirit tumbling through the vast universe. If we view our animal companions from the vantage of spirit, their passing will evoke our gratitude and we can draw from the experience a sense of peace, even joy, that outweighs the sorrow.

For many the thought of losing an animal companion looms ominously large, long before the actual fact must be faced. How often I hear variations on this theme: "I don't know what I'll do when Rover dies; I just can't bear to think of losing him," or "I'll never get another dog. I'm already upset by the thought of Muffy dying and she's not even sick! I just couldn't go through the pain again."

Gently, I respond: *Let go.* So easy to say. But easy to carry out? We so often associate letting go with the pain and fear of losing. Therein lies the difficulty. But letting go is not losing. Rather, it is "loosing," a vastly different concept. To let go is to discover the magic of now.

All beings in nature celebrate the now. All, that is, except human beings. We worry about the future or bury ourselves in the past. If we could but be in tune with today and celebrate with our animals. Stand back from them and observe. Let them be exactly who they are. Learn from them; grow with them. And know that when the time comes for them to move on, they will leave blessed, while we remain enriched.

Although the animal world abounds with a treasure trove of special creatures, resources of opportunity, each with their individual purpose, my story mainly concerns dogs. I know dogs and they know me. They allow me into their world—a wise world of love and joy. These wonderful creatures round out my life. Companionship and devotion clearly characterize the human-dog relationship. Our mutual bonds are deep and beautiful. A lifetime of experiences with my dogs has opened a window of understanding through which I observe a unique view, a tableau of opportunity for learning and growth. Whimsically and intuitively going about their lives, my companions teach me to love, to trust, to let go.

My journey embraces many dogs and covers many years of growth involving both joy and pain. You will meet some of the dogs here who warmed and shaped my path, contributing to the overall awakening of my consciousness. Even my earliest memories recall the sense of discovery I felt as various characteristics of these special animals manifested. Over time I began to view the life and death experiences of my pets in a new light. I wondered about the "universal soul" or spirit as it related to animals. So many qualities animals represent—love, loyalty, goodness, humility—are alive, universal, and immortal.

A distinct awareness of an ongoing spiritual nature in animals emerged as my experiences with my pets evolved. I considered the millions of people who had adopted animals as their home companions and who suffered when their beloved pet died. Could they be comforted by a similar vision of beyond? My personal experiences nurtured a strong desire in me to help, to transmit to others the love, the hope, and the sense of opportunity for personal growth I have known with my animals. As my journey unfolds here, it is my desire to transform our often-tragic responses to the deaths of our animal friends into grateful appreciation for those lives—appreciation filled with understanding, comfort, and hope.

A JOURNEY TOGETHER

Loving and Sharing

*I am Joy in a woolly coat
come to dance into your life
to make you laugh!*

Shadow

1

Shadow

Shadow followed my peanut butter sandwich home, ensconced herself in our hearts, and remained with us for thirteen beautiful years. This lovely, black Lab-Setter embodied her name from the start. Following our every move, asking for attention, and giving and receiving love occupied a major part of her day. Her penchant for food caused an accident which led to our first family council and a discussion about animals and their care I remember to this day.

Shadow's investigative nose created the crisis. Exploring the open refrigerator as a teen-age party got under way, the puppy found herself in the middle of bustling activity. Pushed aside, she slipped on the floor, fell through an open door and down the basement stairs, and broke her leg. Some boys attending the party took the injured pup to emergency care. My father met them there and after consulting with the doctors, returned home and called the family together. My six-year-old ears paid sober attention to the formidable issues he raised.

He knew we wanted to ensure a quality life for Shadow. The severe break offered no certainty of that. My father questioned our willingness—and ability—to meet the responsibility of her care, especially if she did not mend properly. As we discussed her plight, Shadow lay in the hospital under heavy sedation.

"Wouldn't it be kinder to let her continue to sleep, not ever wakening to her pain?" my father gently suggested. I still remember rejecting that notion with all my being. I determined to save her young life. We all pleaded and promised to do our part if a possibility of her recovering existed.

My father acquiesced, Shadow underwent surgery, and she came home, dragging her pink cast behind her. Though tentative at first, she showed no sign of pain. From that day forward, she grew stronger and stronger and never again suffered ill effects from the ordeal.

A gentling and softening takes place in an animal after it undergoes a trauma, perhaps because it experiences its own vulnerability. Undoubtedly, the loving care it receives while recovering contributes to that process. Shadow gave gentleness and drew her own measure from us for the rest of her life.

Within the first two years of Shadow's long life with us she gave birth to two litters of nine puppies each! As Shadow's first birthing day approached, Mother prepared a clean, cozy spot for her upstairs, where the dog could be easily attended to. Mother Nature and Shadow chose otherwise. The basement laundry chute provided the swaddling clothes for these pups, and the assistance Shadow required took place on that basement floor.

No matter to me and my brother and sisters. We were witnessing a miracle. It was the most beautiful sight I'd ever seen. Were these squirming, squeaking, shapeless forms really going to be dogs? In a few short weeks it appeared so. They graduated from mother's milk to solids from a muffin tin—a comical display as the larger and stronger puppies elbowed their way from cup to cup and had to be restrained and retrained.

They all thrived and, to the admiration of the neighborhood, gained weight and beauty. When the puppies were old enough to be placed in homes we advertised them for sale. All the puppies found homes and we divided the profits among us—our first earnings! From that first litter I remember Saddle best—a white duplicate of Shadow with a black saddle across his back. Saddle went to a home near my school and so I saw him often. I enjoyed watching him grow into a handsome, winning chap.

A year later we moved to the country and there Shadow conceived a second litter. Once again nine barely recognizable creatures spilled into the world and our hearts. When it came time for their departure to new homes we said goodbye to eight very respectable dogs. A very loveable but not terribly handsome black-and-white male remained with us. Named "Mugwump" for his distinctive face and rather large posterior, he settled in to being the second dog of the family. It did not take long before he surpassed Shadow in size and energy. A friendly, happy youngster, Mugs tackled life exuberantly.

However, his friendliness was also his eventual undoing. Mugs did not appear for dinner one evening. In scouring the immediate area for him we learned that he had followed a neighbor boy as he rode his bike into town. He was eventually outdistanced and the boy thought he would return home. We never saw Mugwump again.

As I look back on those long-ago days I think again about Mugs and our efforts to find him. We were a responsible and caring family. Yet I wonder: did we do all that we could to find and protect that young dog? What would we do differently today?

I think there has been a consciousness shift regarding animal friends. For one thing, we do not allow dogs to roam freely as we did then. Also, a network for finding lost pets exists today. I do not think that was the case when Mugwump ran off. Yes, I wonder about Mugs. I feel very uncomfortable when I think of him.

Shadow did not give birth again and she remained our only dog until her death. Ultimately, a progressive cancer caused her unbearable pain and we knew unequivocally her time had come. We experienced both grief and relief on that difficult day. A painless death stilled Shadow's suffering. We, however, were left behind to deal with the loss of our dear friend.

As a young child, I had witnessed the death of our first family dog, Toro, under the wheels of a truck. I do not remember the dog well, yet the horrifying scene of his death stayed with me for years and left me with a lasting impression: the death of an animal means finality. At nineteen I still held that view. Shadow's life was over; Shadow, too, was gone forever.

Andy

2

Andy

Shadow and Mugs had simply come into our lives. However, most people choose their home companion. Many considerations surround that choice. What species or breed? Male or female? What size? Short or long hair? Will it be kept indoors, outdoors, or both? Will it be alone all day? Are there children in the family, and if so, what ages? The list of questions goes on.

Sometimes a spontaneous decision appropriately occurs. You simply know. Our animals often appear to pick us. Perhaps a greater power nudges us toward one another at just the right time, kindling a spark that lights the way to mutual belonging. Maybe a part of ourselves attracts the pet best suited to us, drawing it into our lives to help us develop and grow. Andy, our next dog, was just such an animal.

When Shadow died, my mother felt deep sorrow. However, released from the day to day care of an animal, she expressed her wish not to have another dog for awhile. Her desired respite was short-lived, however.

Grocery shopping on our way home from fall classes, my father and I noticed a posted announcement of free puppies. Sharing an enthusiasm for dogs—necessary components of the family—we decided to stop by the given address on our way home just to "have a look."

Captivating sights and sounds greeted us as six roly-poly, adorable puppies clamored for attention. One thing led to another. Amid the squeals and yelps we chose our favorite of the litter, gained assurance from the owner that we could bring the puppy back if Mother objected to him, bundled the little guy up against the sharp wind of approaching winter, and carried him home to the hearth. There he remained. Mother easily succumbed to his charm. Never once did we entertain a thought of returning him.

An irresistible puppy who resembled a miniature black bear cub, this Labrador-Golden Retriever mix grew into a handsome fellow of almost regal bearing. He shared his birth date with Prince Andrew of England; his mother, named Princess, was a champion Golden. Logically, we called our puppy Andy.

Andy's affectionate nature endeared him to people and he thrived on human contact. I remember being dropped off at home one night by a carload of my friends. With eager anticipation Andy waited to greet us. A gregarious, rough and tumbley chap, he barely acknowledged me as he bounded into the automobile and threw his seventy pounds affably across each lap in the back seat. Unlike my friends, he appeared unperturbed by the ensuing uproar. He radiated buoyant good will and relished sharing it with all!

Andy maintained an independent life, too, creating adventures as he roamed the Wisconsin countryside where we lived. His confident behavior and healthy appearance upon return evidenced his obvious enjoyment of these extra-curricular activities. He galloped back into the yard, head held high, ears blowing back, and even the semblance of a smile on his face. His flowing hair contained souvenirs of the surrounding marsh, woods, and cornfields. Rain or shine, winter or summer, he gave himself over to the joy of being a dog.

I always considered Andy to be "mine" although my college studies and activities occupied much of my time and did not allow for long periods of exclusive attention. He functioned as a family dog who bonded with us all. When he was two years old I moved away from home and sensibly left him in my parents' care. I missed him, yet I always knew I could return home to see him. What joyous and fun filled reunions we enjoyed as we romped about and "exchanged" all the latest news!

Because our get-togethers were not frequent, one might have expected a detachment in my feelings towards Andy. Yet, seven years later, when a call came from home telling me Andy had been euthanized because of cancer, I felt an enormously deep void. Had I been with him I could not have prevented the outcome; nevertheless, I felt cut off and out of control regarding his fate. He was only nine years old, too young to die.

Grief and emptiness consumed me; I was inconsolable. Yet, how could this be after seven years of separation? Andy's death had a remarkable impact on me in spite of the physical distance between us. Time and space had not destroyed our bond. As I marveled at this I began to wonder, What *is* this human-animal bond?

Misty

3

Misty

The fall of 1971 brought new experiences and adjustments to my life as I moved into a new apartment in a new city and began a new job. Furthermore, just across the street, a tiny, cuddly puppy that was to become my special companion entered the world. When a hand-lettered cardboard sign reading "Free Puppies" appeared on my neighbors' front lawn, my natural affinity for dogs led me to their door.

What a treat! Four precious, squirmy pups, only six weeks old, spilled over me in abandon. My eyes settled on the smallest of the litter, a little black one with lovely white markings on her chest, feet and the tip of her tail. For a moment, Andy reappeared before my eyes, stirring memories of another fall day.

As I carefully picked up my chosen one, she seemed totally content to snuggle in my arms. That was that. Delightedly, I zipped her into the front of my ski jacket and carried her back across the street to her new home.

Looking into her tiny black eyes, I realized they were still cloudy, or misty. "Misty," I said aloud. "Yes, Misty is your name."

Relearning the art of raising a puppy, an often frustrating and very tiring task, soon occupied my time. Exercising infinite patience, I learned more quickly than she. From her house training to her outdoor routines I worked with her, devoting all my free time to her development. Every noon, I rushed home from my teaching job to take her outside. We played ball briefly, took a walk and then parted until the after-school hours. As I turned to wave goodbye, I melted at the sight of her face in the window watching wistfully. Usually she perched on the back of my sofa in the living room; this habit soon spoiled its fresh, new look. I learned later that keeping her confined to a much smaller space would have ensured a more secure feeling for her as well as preserved my belongings.

As Misty grew bigger she needed extended exercise periods, so I scheduled daily jaunts around a nearby lake. She learned to stay in control on and off her leash. I perceived her own sense of pride as she behaved "properly" and was praised for doing so. Whenever I could, I took her with me for a ride in the car, a treat she came to expect and love. The very jingle of the car keys signaled her. Off she'd scamper, beating me to the car door. She filled a need for me and I found myself becoming very attached to her. Moreover, we were a team!

At the time I was not aware of what I would refer to today as an unhealthy aspect of my attachment to Misty. On the surface we presented a winning picture, my dog and I. In reality I relied exclusively on Misty to provide the security I so needed at that time. Looking back now,

I realize what a strain such reliance imposes on the human-animal bond, both for the person and the animal involved. Exclusivity, which leaves little room for others, human or animal, cannot be a part of a healthy bond. Later repercussions affirmed this truth.

Within a year I married and moved to a more countrified, hilly part of the city, an area with open space, perfect for a dog of Misty's size. By then she had grown into a fairly large Labrador type, a "California Lab" some called her, never saying exactly what that meant. A pretty gal, she was. We introduced her to the beach and enjoyed frequent outings on the sand and rocks, where Misty chased the gulls or bravely took on the waves. When at home she spent her days in pleasurable pursuits—scurrying through the field next door, rooting out its varied inhabitants, chasing a hand-tossed tennis ball, or simply lolling about, enjoying her home and our companionship. Life flowed idyllically.

Misty and Lady

4

Liberated Lady

As I curiously perused the pet column of the newspaper one evening this ad drew my attention:

Free puppy to good home, 5 months. Half St. Bernard, half Australian Sheep. Excellent with children, has shots. NEEDS LOVE.

I read the ad to my husband who responded, "That's all we need—a St. Bernard!" It took him about ten minutes to suggest that I at least call. Thinking *why not*, I dialed the number and a short time later we had an appointment to meet this free five-month-old puppy.

"Libby" arrived the next day, freckles on her nose, pink bows adorning her ears. Propelled by a ridiculous romp, she happily investigated her new surroundings. Barely pausing for introduction, she and Misty cavorted together excitedly. Misty thought she was just great and my husband seemed quite taken with this bouncing bundle of fluff. She did not, however, charm me. As the dogs played together, Libby's "people" told us of her history.

Born July 31, 1972, "Liberated Lady" was the ninth and last pup of a San Francisco Saint Bernard mother and an Australian Shepherd father. Pushed aside by her litter mates, this small and sickly puppy was literally nursed into life by her owners with a diet of special stews, vitamins, and above all, love. Exercised regularly, she grew...and grew...and grew. What a sight she must have been as she walked her owners through the city streets carrying her leash in her mouth, a practice she maintained for the rest of her life. It soon became apparent that she was too big for a city apartment. Thus, in January, 1973 her owners placed the newspaper ad.

By that time I was totally and singularly attached to Misty. Although we lived in a perfect location to raise more than one dog, I felt unsure about sharing my affections with another canine creature. My exclusive love for Misty had a clinging, possessive quality. So it was with apprehension that I agreed to a trial adoption of this liberated lady.

Naming a dog establishes its identity as well as creating a link of communication. The name Libby didn't suit our new dog, yet a better choice eluded us. Needing to call her something, we began to use the second part of her given name, calling her simply Lady. Very soon, our dilemma became academic; her name was the least of our problems. In addition to Lady's apparent lack of house training, she didn't seem to understand or respond to a thing we said. Nothing registered—her former name, her new name, simple commands. Even our greetings went unnoticed. She acted happy and related well to Misty but seemed to be utterly untrainable. No longer was the new dog on trial; she *was* a trial—and we felt stuck. In frustration I tried to reach her original owners. No luck. I next took her to our veterinarian for advice and a check-up—a most revealing visit!

Lady bore a problem greater than ours. She totally lacked hearing, a condition which had probably existed from birth. This news altered my attitude toward the dog. My feelings softened as I considered communicating with her, although I placed her needs secondary to my own will and desires. Visually, through hand signals and facial expressions, I "told" her what to do and when to do it. Smiling, arms opened wide inviting embrace, I showed my pleasure. Conversely, a very stern look adequately admonished her.

All the while Lady expressed herself to me also, through an entirely different means. Her important messages—trust, loyalty, unconditional love—were offered in silence across a wavelength I chose to disregard. I truly resisted her and she somehow knew I was not quite in tune with her.

Misty and Lady, however, were in complete harmony. They seemed to have developed their own sense of exchange. I wondered if Misty perceived Lady's deafness or if she operated from her position as number-one dog. I watched her show the younger dog the ropes. Follow-the-leader was the name of their game. Misty chose their times for play and initiated rest periods. Where to run? Misty's choice again. Wherever they went, Misty led and Lady scrambled after her, occasionally eliciting peals of laughter from observers as Misty outmaneuvered the less agile pup.

On one such occasion, Misty proceeded across a

mountain stream. Like a gazelle, she leapt into the air, sailed over the water and landed cleanly on the other side. Lady followed. Kerplunk! She missed the opposite bank altogether. Totally abashed, she climbed out of the water sporting only a bruised ego.

Occasionally Misty gallivanted through the neighborhood, taking Lady with her. I imagined her greeting all she passed as if to say, "This is my new sister. We've come to play!" When Lady picked up her leash, her way of asking to go for a walk, Misty grabbed the other end, changing the game to tug-of-war. In this silent, playful communication their bond grew strong.

Somehow we weathered Lady's trial period and she stayed without our ever discussing her transition from trial to acceptance. My husband, his three children who were in and out, myself, the two dogs, and our cat all settled into a typical family routine.

About that time we acquired a VW bus with a sunroof. A platform bed in the bus provided space for both the dogs and kids to ride and we all enjoyed the fun of traveling to the beach, the mountains, or across the country. Even a trip to the market became an occasion for the dogs to ride in the bus. They expected and relished each excursion.

Misty soon discovered the pleasure of poking her head through the open sunroof. Feet planted firmly on the platform, she could just reach the opening with her front paws. From that position she commanded a spectacular view. Lady's bulk prevented her from experiencing the same joy. She contented herself by occupying the front seat and hanging her chin on the side window frame, allowing the rushing air to blow her ears back. Aware of the ever present danger of some foreign object flying in their faces, I discouraged the practice and yet occasionally, against my better judgement, I gave in. They certainly were an amusing sight to behold!

One day, as we headed for the toll gate of the Bay Bridge, Lady decided to "taste" the curtains in the bus. All in one instant I discovered her mischief, threw my most powerful disciplinary look her way, and watched helplessly as she leapt through the open window into the oncoming traffic. Escaping my wrath, she quickly scurried across five lanes of highway. My only recourse was to stop the bus, try to halt the oncoming cars, and cajole Lady into returning. My particular hand signal for "come" was to pat my chest with both hands and that is just what I did, adding my sweetest "come-hither" smile.

What a hilarious scene! The pantomime commanded full attention and traffic came to a halt. Once Lady decided it was safe to return to me, she slowly sashayed back to the bus, none the worse for her escapade. Horns tooted, motorists waved, and we continued on our way.

Lady

5

Death in a New Light

Early in June, 1975, our tranquillity crumbled abruptly. Because I harbored concern about the dogs roaming freely, particularly with my possessive feelings towards Misty, we fenced in our yard. Apparently Misty panicked when we drove off one evening leaving her enclosed in the yard, for she "escaped" and set out to look for us. We were gone only a short time, yet we found no Misty upon return. I called and I searched both by foot and by car. No dog. In my heart I think I knew the chilling truth—Misty was not coming back. I didn't want to believe it.

I went to bed that night with a heavy, fearful dread clutching at me. At midnight I sat straight up, alert, in a state of alarm. Sensing Misty, I ran to the front gate. An eerie, empty silence greeted me. At dawn, after a fitful night's sleep, I resumed my search again.

Knowing Misty's collar and tags would identify her, I returned home periodically to see if anyone had called, telling me where I could pick her up. On one of those stops I encountered my husband's anguished face and the words I couldn't bear to hear, "She's not coming home, Julie. We've had a call. Misty's dead."

Today, eleven years later, I can still recall the uncontrolled disbelief and rage that tore through me that Sunday morning. Misty had been hit by a car and was found by the Animal Control. "Sometime last night," they said. They didn't say what time. Could it have been midnight? Had I indeed "known" in some way when I abruptly wakened and ran to the gate? How furious I was at those who hit her! How angered with those who took her away without my seeing her. How guilty I felt that I hadn't been with her, hadn't somehow prevented this. In fact, I assumed responsibility for causing her death by fencing in the yard. I was shattered!

Misty's departure was the third traumatic loss I had experienced in two years. Earlier, the deaths of two close childhood friends had churned my emotions and raised sobering questions about life and death. My spiritual background provided me with some understanding and comfort in handling the grief I felt. I believed their souls had moved on to a beautiful, joyous reunion with our Creator. An eternity of peace and happiness enfolded them.

I had never seen the death of an animal in the same light. Previously my animals' deaths, though sad and even painful, did not inspire a search for deeper meaning. When Misty died I explored for the first time the meaning of life and death in a nonhuman but equally vital form. I wondered, did that car accident totally end Misty's life? Was her life contained solely in her body's form? My intuition, hampered by the numbing effect of grief, struggled to define the elusive truth. My mind blurred as questions continued to arise.

Looking back, I realize how I used the anger and frustration of my grief to exclude Lady. She was going through her own grief process and deserved better, yet she experienced my resentment that she, not Misty, still lived. Lady spent hours and days waiting at the top of the road for her friend to return. Each night, when no bark of recognition had been uttered, no greeting had been exchanged, she shuffled back to the house and curled up alone in sadness, watching. She continually observed me, lovingly, patiently waiting for a spark of recognition from me that would tell her, "You are accepted and loved just as you are, because you are."

I spent time compiling a scrapbook of pictures, chronicling Misty's life, keeping her alive in my heart. Gradually, in the next few weeks, I reached out somewhat to Lady. Aware of her hurt, a part of me looked to her to heal my own sense of loss. To her delight, we went for rides and walks together, just the two of us. I made a point of reaching out to pet her; the touching soothed us both. Yes, opportunity was raising its gentle, prodding voice once again.

Lady and Perro

6

Perro

I resolved to avoid ever experiencing again the pain I knew in losing Misty. Yet, only a month after her death I began to scan the pet column in the newspaper, once again looking for black Labs. An ad for a "black Lab puppy, male, 8 weeks old" caught my eye. Making an initial inquiry, I learned that two local women took in stray or homeless dogs, had them checked by a veterinarian, boarded them at the vet's, and advertised their availability as pets. I decided to visit them and meet the pup.

Perhaps my general unreceptivity closed my mind to this puppy. He simply did not appeal to me. His caretaker suggested that before I leave I meet another of their "finds," a young male, mixed breed, whom they had recently discovered hiding in a local city sewer system!

A gangly Lab-Shepherd-Dobie-looking puppy came slipping and sliding into the room and ended spread-eagled on the slippery hospital floor. What a wiggly sight—36 x 36 x 36—a yard tall, he weighed no more than thirty-six pounds, and displayed a thirty-six-inch tail, or so it seemed. Overjoyed to be the focal point of our attention, he whipped this extraordinary appendage about with enthusiasm.

Something else about him captured my attention as well. As he playfully cuffed the smaller puppy and rolled on his back to allow the little one to crawl all over him, I found his gentle manner very fetching. I agreed to take him home on trial.

Lady was waiting in the bus for me. Her initial pleasure at seeing me return soured as the alien pup invaded her territory. She moved into the farthest corner and glowered in his direction. Only a mile or so down the road he, too, felt less than happy. Apparently he had experienced little, if any, auto travel and his system handled the ride poorly. Lady was indignant. She jumped over my car seat and wedged her seventy-five-pound fluffy body between me and the door. I could not budge her. For five miles I inched along, not daring to push the speedometer beyond ten mph. Eventually we arrived home frazzled but safe.

As a former teacher of English as a Second Language, accustomed to conversing in Spanish, I occasionally slipped into that language at home. When I spoke to the puppy in this foreign vernacular, he responded with visible recognition, cocking his head to the side and perking up his ears. I referred to him as my new little perro and then simply as Perro. He soon passed his trial and was accepted into our lives, in spite of the sting I carried in my heart over the loss of Misty.

Practically from that first day, I felt Perro sensed a mission, some special purpose for being in my life. He exhibited a devoted gentleness and an intuitive sense that went beyond his canine form. When I grieved for Misty, as if on cue, Perro would approach me and rest his head on my lap, demanding nothing and offering love. I discovered I had only to think of him and he would be at my side. If I intended to take him with me when going out, he would be at the door before me. If I intended to leave him home, he would not move or even look up as I said goodbye. Sometimes I tested him, saying "stay" when I really meant to take him along. He was never fooled. Perro demonstrated an entirely new kind of communication. In his eyes I perceived qualities beyond animal instinct; neither were they "human" attributes. They spoke of a noble character with an unusual, universal dimension.

As our interaction evolved, growing into a mutual attraction and bond, a relationship between Lady and Perro was also developing. A curious phenomenon unfolded. Just as Lady had come under Misty's tutelage, Perro was subject to Lady's instruction. In spite of her handicap, Lady took the lead, putting the youngster through his paces. Wherever she led, he followed. She taught him to tug at the leash she carried in her mouth by placing it in his and, with him firmly attached, pulling him around.

When he misbehaved, which was often, she reacted to his exuberant lack of discipline by being a model of perfection, as if to say, "Pay attention, if you wish to have a harmonious home life!" She took great pride in pleasing me with her exemplary behavior. She would romp over to me and thrust her St. Bernard bulk against me, nuzzling affectionately, always with one eye on Perro, making sure he noticed. Probably time and maturity were as instrumental as Lady in helping Perro shape up.

Still, her steady, loving nature and ever-increasing acceptance of the newcomer laid the foundation for what became a close friendship between them.

Perro continued to warm that spot in my heart reserved for Misty and I staunchly defended him to others in my family who became exasperated with his behavior. I often told him, "You've had a difficult role to fill and you're handling it mighty well." He performed all the antics of growing up as a dog should and at the same time, as he gazed at me, he seemed to reach into my being. I sensed in him a very special and rare quality of understanding. It captivated me.

Lady carried on in her own way—awkward, funny, and loving. For some reason, however, a barrier still remained between us. Although I took care of her on a day to day basis, I withheld that extra measure. I was not yet aware of her eventual importance in my life. She continued to be my husband's favorite and fortunately claimed considerable attention and affection from him.

Dollar Bill

7

Dollar Bill and Change

I n 1976, disruption struck again. Within the space of six months, I experienced three tragic losses—the deaths of my father and two more dear friends. My father's death was unexpected, the result of a car accident. It triggered shock and intense sadness but also great love and solidarity in the family and community. Each of my friends suffered from forms of cancer. I was privileged to spend time with them both prior to their deaths, to share in their wisdom and, indeed, joy as they prepared for their transitions. However, the emotions I experienced at losing three people close to me took me to a brink.

I retreated into myself, searching for answers to unstated questions, trying to cope. I handled the stress poorly. Outwardly I seemed to manage but inwardly I felt very vulnerable and unhappy. No longer teaching school, I had time on my hands and too many things to think about. I turned to my animals. I "told" them how I felt, confided in them, and lavished attention on them.

In the midst of these wrenching experiences, a workable idea for occupying my time and energy came to me. Traveling or otherwise absentee dog owners needed a secure, loving "home away from home" for their animals. Bringing other dogs into our environs was both possible and practical. Why not? The word went out, calls came in and the dogs began to appear.

It turned out this was a popular service! Dogs soon inundated the place and I loved it. A nurturing, caring side of my personality was spending itself on these creatures and we experienced mutual rewards. The "parents" loved it, too. Whenever FSBO, all-time super Poodle—intelligent, handsome, and spoiled—arrived for a visit, his master hoisted him on one shoulder, joined him for a chorus of song, and then deposited him on the other side of the gate, saying, "So long, FSBO. Have a good time at camp!" Indeed he did! He moved right in and I grew very fond of him. Today he counts this as his second home.

All the dogs, permanent residents and visitors, interacted harmoniously, although Lady began to manifest a degree of jealousy. She had the silliest way of eyeing the object of her desire or discontent. With her droopy St. Bernard eyes she stared determinedly until someone took notice. If that someone happened to be a visiting dog, a growl was added to the charade. "Queen of the Roost" she proclaimed herself, allowing no one to forget it.

One of our regular house guests was an adorable Cock-a-poo named Dollar Bill. Dollar belonged to a woman whose job as flight attendant took her out of town frequently. Seeing my ad for home pet care brought her right over to meet us. Judy and I took to one another instantly and very soon thereafter the dogs welcomed Dollar into the fold.

What a package of fun! Dollar reflected Judy's *joie de vivre*. He felt good about himself and expected us to like him. No chore that! He didn't just enter a room, he bounded in full of spunk, tail wagging in double time, big brown eyes sparkling. Often he carried a tennis ball in his mouth which he ceremoniously placed at my feet, expecting me to toss it for him to retrieve. He became as much a part of the family as Lady and Perro, involving himself in all the activities that had become our routine. My developing friendship with Judy became a special by-product of "dog-sitting." Life appeared to be going well.

My inner world still suffered, however, as did my relationship with my husband. With much sadness we acknowledged our unhappiness and agreed to separate. This difficult time affected Lady, also. She missed her friend. A new and disturbing behavior began to assert itself—insecurity, purposeful wrong doing, demands on my time. I finally reached my wits' end. My husband, in no position to take her himself, suggested I find a new home for her or have her put to sleep[1] if I really couldn't cope with the stress. His words jarred my sensibilities.

From a new perspective, I took stock of the blessings of my situation. My animal family offered me an opportunity to learn. Our reciprocal relationship involved giving and receiving. My attitude toward Lady changed

---

[1]Although this term is part of the common vernacular, it would be far better to avoid its usage altogether. Children often do not comprehend its true implications for they relate sleeping to awakening. The consequences can be very damaging.

and I became receptive to the animals teaching me their secrets of patience and joy. In their world of nonverbal communication, the dogs seemed to agree to bring happiness and interest into my life again. Lady's behavior improved immeasurably as she, Perro, the kitty, and I relaxed in mutual enjoyment.

Benny

8

Pride 'N' Groom

D ollar Bill and other "boarders" continued to be part-time residents. Dollar's maintenance included shampoos and haircuts at a professional grooming salon, an establishment unfamiliar to me. Such comical behavior he exhibited after being groomed! On one hand, as he rolled about on his back, snorting and huffing, he seemed determined to "rub off" that sissy stuff—the fragrance, hairdo, the whole works. On the other hand, he proudly strutted about showing off his newly pampered body, his sense of self-esteem highly visible. That an animal sensed its appearance piqued my interest and I decided to study dog grooming.

My private lessons required a model. My neighbor, Al, laughed when I asked if I might borrow his dog, Scruffy, a terrier befitting her name. Nevertheless, he agreed, and my training began. Scruffy should have received a patience award for what she endured as I slowly learned and practiced the finer points of grooming. "That's not my dog!" cried Al a few weeks later when a transformed Scruffy came home sporting cologne and a modified Schnauzer trim. Scruffy and I, however, thought she was a pretty fine example of her undefined breed.

Upon graduating from Scruffy I accompanied my teacher to her regular job. There, under her supervision, I groomed every conceivable type of dog. Soon, I knew enough to venture out on my own. I temporarily assisted an experienced and very capable groomer in her shop, planting the seeds of a new career and establishing the nucleus for a whole new set of friends, both human and canine.

With new skill and some tools, I pursued the goal of opening my own grooming business. Calling my enterprise Pride 'N' Groom, I printed some flyers and set out to make my name known. For people who needed to have their dogs groomed but had difficulty getting their pets to the grooming salon, I offered an individual approach—dog grooming at my home with optional pick-up and delivery. Through various veterinary hospitals and friends of friends, I contacted pet owners of all ages who were delighted and supportive of my venture. For several of my older customers, I represented vital reassurance that their beloved pet, often their sole companion and an integral part of their lives, would receive loving care and even a new home if they became ill or passed on. Just knowing they could leave my name with their family or neighbor eased their concerns.

Gradually Pride 'N' Groom became a thriving and stimulating way of life, with new people contacting me all the time. Hairdos varied from Sir Lancelot's elegant coiffure to Charlie Chan's bi-monthly restoration. I thoroughly enjoyed all aspects of my job and especially delighted in my woolly friends—Dilly, Stuffin', Heidi, Wiggles, Popcorn, Sophie, Raki, Angus, Calypso—and the list goes on. So many dogs to love and learn from!

One of my new friends, a beautiful Irish Setter-Collie puppy, belonged to an elderly customer. The dog's silky, tricolored coat—black, tan, and white with lovely markings—shone glossy and fine. The active, untrained pup escaped to the street many times, narrowly missing being hit in the busy traffic. Finally, the pound picked him up. The owner's nephew contacted me. His aunt could no longer care for the dog, and therefore he was available to me if I wanted to give him a home. This delighted me for I had become very fond of the dog in a short period of time. I immediately drove to the pound to pick him up.

The ordeal of enclosure in a restricted space obviously had frightened him. When the handlers brought him out to me, he dashed for cover into a crawl space under the shelter. In spite of my white slacks I slithered after him and dragged him out. What a pair we were! Whispering gentle persuasion into his ear, I just barely managed to get him into the car. Once in, however, he sat up straight as an arrow on the front seat and off we went. He looked magnificent!

A talk show on the car radio brought in a call from a person named Ben. I dubbed my new untrained and unnamed pet Benny then and there. As we pulled into the driveway at home, Lady and Perro greeted Benny in the usual manner, with curiosity, much barking, and apparent acceptance. Benny settled into the household routine quickly and easily.

Within days, the dogs established a mutual camaraderie. I watched with delight as they entertained one another. Bobbing and weaving, pouncing and prancing, they played together. Color-wise, the dogs presented a visual treat. Predominantly black, Perro and Benny shared nearly identical markings, although Ben's long, flowing hair distinguished him. Lady, mostly white, provided interesting contrast.

The three of them adopted my sometimes overwhelming desire to go to the ocean, to exhilarate in the power of the crashing waves, to run on the beach, to take in the stinging salt air, to feel totally free and alive. Lady's acute sense of smell compensated for her lack of hearing. It was she who announced to the troops that we were headed for the beach as she took in the scent and nearly went frantic with excitement. Upon arrival at the shore, she led the entourage as they tore from the car and raced across the sand. Their carefree, innocent exuberance was infectious. All around, people stopped to watch and smiled. Remembering that scene today brings joy to my heart.

Benny loved to "talk." He tended to take over the scene when he wanted to communicate, which was most of the time. I found myself giving him excessive and exclusive attention, to the confusion of the other dogs. Perro, in particular, would stand off to the side and watch me, a quizzical look on his face. In forming this strong attachment to Benny, I actually set the stage for a difficult but extremely important lesson I would be given to work through—how to let go. I do not suggest that my feelings caused the chain of events that were to follow; only that the opportunity to grow through overcoming pain was all the more dramatic for my having attached so strongly to this splendid animal.

Perro and Lady

9

Benny

Late one night I came home to find both Lady and Perro waiting at the front gate to welcome me, strangely apprehensive. "Where's Benny?" I inquired. In answer, Perro whined and pawed at the ground. I began to call Ben and heard him cry in response. Thinking the sound came from an adjacent field, I started down the steep hill in the dark, calling to him as I stumbled along. Each call received an answer but every response seemed to come from a greater distance. I ran back up the hill, got into my car, and set out searching and calling. His feeble cries led me down the road to where I found him, lying in a ditch, unable to move.

"Oh, Benny," I cried. "Why?" Almost apologetically, he licked my hand. A passing motorist kindly stopped and helped me transfer the injured dog to my car. How grateful I will always be for his loving assistance and concern.

I'll never know how Benny got out of my yard. Nor will I know what hit him. Although he was wearing identification tags bearing his name, address, and telephone number, I never received any word as to what actually took place. I do know that despite emergency treatment that night and further care the next day with my regular veterinarian and friend, Benny was irreversibly injured. He sustained multiple fractures of his back, legs, and tail. He would never walk again and would be incontinent. Although his vital signs were good they alone could not ensure a decent life for him.

I knew what I must do and I didn't know how I could go through with it. My cousin, Kate, counselled me: "He must not know that you're upset. He counts on you for strength and love. He deserves that now." And so the next day I took his favorite "cookies" in to him, sat and petted him and talked to him. Bless his heart. He wanted to get up and sit for his treats as he had been taught, but he was unable to do so.

The time had come. With as much gentleness and calm as I could muster, I told Benny that it was time to go to bed. He protested mildly and then, trusting, he obeyed and put his head down. He showed no fear, no holding on. He passed away peacefully, as the doctor and I patted and soothed him. I thought of the prayer of the great healer, Albert Schweitzer, whose enormous capacity for love and compassion had inspired me and so many others.

> Hear our humble prayer, O God, for our friends, the animals. Especially for animals who are suffering; for any that are hunted or lost or deserted or frightened or hungry; for all that must be put to death. We entreat for them all thy mercy and pity. And for those who deal with them, we ask a heart of compassion, gentle

and kindly words. Make us true friends of the animals
and so to share the blessings of the merciful.

God gave me the strength I needed at that moment
and added another precious gift, as well. For a year after
Benny's death, I could extend my hand and "feel" his
beautiful, silky coat, just as real as if he stood before me.
Although I no longer reach out, I will never forget how
it felt or how it eased the pain.

A certain sense of triumph carried me through that
traumatic experience. Letting go is never easy, and yet I
involved myself in Benny's death to the ultimate extent
and was able to let him go with dignity and in peace. To
be sure, I felt the stabbing pain of loss but I also knew
reward. A new understanding emerged, although it
would take more time and experience to fully grasp the
truth about possessiveness and letting go.

We live in a world that teaches us to clutch and cling,
yet time and again we learn that this results in emptiness
and loss. During those memorable moments with Benny, I began to turn the focus from myself outward
towards him. Much as I wanted to turn the clock back, to
pretend that the accident had not occurred, I had to
look at his life from his viewpoint. I loved him and that
did not stop in letting go; there is no end to love. On
some level, I realized that letting go of Benny in the
finite was a step towards allowing me to enter into a
greater understanding of the infinite, for when we can
let go of the outer manifestation we open ourselves to
seeing beyond.

Lucy Bill

10

Lucy Bill

Returning home to my "family," I embarked on another beginning. Mindful of the interdependency of all of creation, I wondered why these particular animals were with me and what place they occupied in the larger scheme of things. What could I be doing with, for, or because of them in order to grow and expand? How could my experience and knowledge benefit my customer friends and their pets?

Lady's steady, devoted love, an engaging aspect of her personality, became more evident to me. She waited patiently to be recognized and happily received any kind word or look of acknowledgement. As I watched this gentle creature, a struggle went on within me. With difficulty, I confronted my past attitudes of resentment and indifference towards her and resolved to make it up to her.

Although she enjoyed good health, her nine years represented longevity for a dog of St. Bernard heritage. Each passing year became a gift, a blessing. Gradually, as I accepted each moment and simply enjoyed her, a special love grew. She joined me on grooming days, content to spend her time amid the hustle and bustle of the business as long as she was close to me. She showed remarkable restraint with the intruding clientele. Across her bridge of silence she communicated subtle reminders of the proper scheme of things; I belonged to her and all guests were a necessary annoyance.

Perro, too, settled into an easy relationship with me, Lady, and Sammy Cat. If he experienced rejection because of my preoccupation with Benny, he showed no signs of harbored resentment, once again demonstrating the forgiving quality of unconditional love our animals clearly and repeatedly exhibit. In fact, Perro stayed very close to me over the next few weeks. The night of Ben's accident had made a strong impression on him. A sensitive dog by nature, the cries he heard that night affected him deeply. He did not leave the yard willingly for many months. I wondered what his thoughts and instincts told him. How did his brain portend danger? Certainly his behavior pattern changed. The secret sense of understanding he had shown before in subtle ways surfaced again, mystifying and fascinating me.

Some three years after Benny's death, we added to our family once again. As I approached the local market late one evening, I noticed several employees huddled by a dog cage, the kind the airlines use for animal transportation. Peering curiously over their shoulders, I discovered the object of their attention: a scruffy, smelly, adorable black puppy with enormous brown eyes. She had apparently been dumped there in her cage early that same day, no note or owners in sight.

"Do you want her?" the employees asked. "Would you give her a home? Do you know anyone who would?"

I steeled myself. "No, no, and no," I replied, and went about my business. About a third of the way down the first aisle I decided I would take her with me, groom her and try to place her in a home if no one else wanted her. At 9:30 p.m. the puppy, her cage, and I left the market. Fifteen minutes later found her slipping about in my doggy tub and shortly thereafter succumbing to the clippers. By 10:30 p.m. she had firmly established herself as the newest member of the fold. What choice had I? She took one look around and said, "Oh my, this is quite nice, thank you. I think I'll stay!"

Now, one-and-a-half years later, she is a very respectable two-year-old Cocker Spaniel who still sleeps in her cage (now called a bed). Unlike my other pets she actually plays with toys. Among her elaborate array, rubber ducky claims favorite-toy status. She carries it about for hours on end, happily offering it to any human visitors, while jealously guarding it from her canine cohorts. She proudly wears a red bandanna about her neck, a contrast to her lovely, shiny black coat. Although afflicted with a terminal case of cuteness, she shows remarkable adjustment to her plight. A happy dog, her body language communicates joy, especially her entire hindquarters which are perpetually in motion. In both looks and personality she closely resembles Dollar Bill, whose untimely death in 1984 broke our hearts. Although called Lucy before we reached home that first night, she now answers to Lucy Bill.

The ongoing years brought many, many dogs to our doorstep for grooming, boarding, and observing. The insight gained with Benny gently nudged me. I appreciated the dogs' special qualities without being totally wrapped up in the animals themselves. Often people asked me how they all managed to get along so well. "They're expected to!" I answered. Truly, I did expect harmony and the animals never let me down. Receiving loving care and trust, they seemed to promote love and trustworthiness.

Lady's moments of jealousy surfaced occasionally. Yet, a mere look or a finger wagging in her direction, much as one would discipline a small child, suppressed her less-than-polite inclinations towards our visitors. She knew my expectations and made pleasing me a first priority, even if it meant swallowing her insecurity. When I praised her for handling the situation in a proper manner, she swelled with pride.

The grooming years provided a great deal of time alone, time to think, during which myriad questions surfaced. I looked within myself for answers to life's mysteries, listening for that still, small voice to tell me so much of what I wanted to know. Focusing inward, I actually turned outward, expanding my inquiry. I began to look at animals in a new way, not just as pets but as a life force. What constitutes this life force? I wondered. Can it be called the spirit that moves through all of life? Is that spirit the same regardless of form, either human or animal? Why am I in one form and animals in another? What is the significance of spirit as it pertains to life and death? Is death the other side of the reality called life or is it an ongoing stage of life? I pondered. And then a very moving experience took place. I felt a spirit move through me and my dog, leaving in its wake suggestions of answers to some of these powerful questions.

Lady

11

Transition

One July morning in 1985 I rather frantically pushed myself to finish my grooming chores in order to attend an afternoon lecture, the final of a summer series. For some unknown reason, Lady remained in the house, not accompanying me to the grooming area. That was just as well, for I felt very pressured. When I completed my work, I barely acknowledged the dogs as I took a long distance call, changed clothes, grabbed a bite to eat, and raced off to the afternoon function. A lengthy question-answer period followed the two-hour talk and an opportunity to say goodbye to the popular lecturer kept me even longer. It was late afternoon when I returned home and found my extremely sick, bloated Lady.

During the next few days I relived those long hours away from Lady over and over again, trying to put them in perspective. I wondered if my lack of attention had exacerbated her problem. Or had she needed to be alone? It seemed to me that a greater hand than mine had been in charge of both Lady's and my activities that day, directing each detail with infinite care. Animals in the wild are known to go away into solitude as death approaches. I believe that Lady somehow knew that her transition, her passing, had begun. Our separation was in order.

Upon arriving home, I knew something was terribly wrong. Lady appeared to be in great pain and unable to support her weight. A phone call to the veterinarian confirmed the urgency of her situation and we took off for the hospital. Almost immediately upon arrival she was taken into surgery to relieve a gastric bloat. The top priority was to clear her stomach. Her apparently fierce will to live helped her survive that first critical procedure. She needed to be monitored all night and I wanted to do that, so later that evening I returned to Lady's side.

Sleep eluded me that night as I alternately tended to Lady and retreated into my own being. I blessed the opportunity this vigil offered, the opportunity to administer the tenderness and care to Lady that I had withheld in earlier years. Throughout the awesome stillness of that night I contemplated Lady's life and my own; I contemplated the Spirit within each of us.

Though different in form, Lady and I partook of life according to our unique beings. Yet the Spirit within each of us transcended our differing forms and personalities. Indeed, Spirit transcends all; it knows no limits, not form or personality, not time or space. As this Spirit energy flows through our many and varied forms we name it Life. What then is death, I thought?

Suddenly, a new and wonderful realization penetrated the night. Death does not mean finality. Death affirms liberation! Death releases all forms of life from their earthly limits. Never before had I considered the other side of an animal's life in this way. I realized that Spirit working through an animal actually frees it—not its personality or form but its "sliver," as it were, of the universal spirit—the part of it that is wisdom, the part that knows its purpose in life, and the part that would have us rejoice in the blessing of our shared lives.

As I pondered this marvelous new insight, Lady stirred at my side and I returned to the consciousness of the here and now. I ran my hand over her sleeping form and listened to her quiet breathing. With new understanding I smiled and closed my eyes in peace.

Lady slept comfortably through the night. The next day, Monday, the doctor expected her to go home. A fever postponed her release, however. Instead of bringing her home, I visited her at the hospital taking her outside for a very slow, shaky walk. We stopped at the car to greet Perro. His ongoing upset at the absence of his friend concerned me. Seeing Lady and rubbing noses with her calmed him. I felt that one more detail of a perfectly orchestrated plan had played its part.

As I visited Lady I knew, though I can't explain how, that she would not be coming home again. When we returned to the hospital after our walk, she "told" me, as clearly as if she had spoken aloud, that she could not go on. Her time had come. I left her to return home, fighting tears, already grieving. Returning to the hospital one more time that night, I was a little startled to find that her fever had subsided and I almost dared to have some hope. The next morning however, the dreaded, though expected call came. She was not doing well. Her liver had been badly damaged by gastric fluid and she was not responding to treatment. I returned to the hospital, taking Perro with me. He lay next to her, offering his affection.

I spent the next two hours holding Lady's head in my hand, petting her and telling her, "It's okay, Lady. You don't need to stay for me. You can go." Over and over, I repeated those words. I prayed with her: "The spirit of God flows freely through Lady, dissolving anything not of itself." And, "I let Lady go to God, peacefully and lovingly." At one point, I thought she no longer knew I was there and I withdrew my hand. Reaching out with her paw, this tender, loving creature drew me back to her.

I didn't want to be in the position of choosing the moment of Lady's death. When it was time, I hoped that she would simply pass on. And that is just what happened. At noon, July 30th, "Liberated Lady" took her last breath and died, one day before her thirteenth birthday. I was profoundly affected. I remember the date and yet at that moment I felt there was no such thing as time. The whole experience took place beyond time, outside of time.

There is a terrible strangeness in saying goodbye to someone you love. I felt hopelessly, helplessly angry. Not towards Lady, certainly, and not towards the wonderful doctors or staff at the hospital. I felt irrational anger towards everyone "out there" who didn't know and therefore couldn't care. I wanted them to care. I wanted everyone to care. "Sweet, wise, loving Lady," I silently sobbed. "Please someone, everyone, mourn her." Of course, some did love Lady. But I knew that most of the response toward her death would be sympathy for me and my loss, not recognition of her beautiful essence I had come to know.

To assuage my grief, I wrote the following tribute to
my friend:

Lady died today.

    that freckled nose ...
       its black tip
          that loved to nuzzle
    that keen sense of smell ...
       announcing to her delight
          we were ocean bound.
    those eyes that somehow
       always looked sad ...
          the alert, expectant
    expression she had
       that said, "I can't hear
          but I can anticipate!"
    the soft, cuddly white fur
       beckoning you ...
          to run your hand through it.
    her funny lope ...
       both hind legs
          running in unison
    to catch up
       to chase a ball,
          a pine cone ...
    oh, those pine cones!
       what a treat they were
          to chase, carry ...
    and then drop
       for me to kick again
          and her to chase ...
    all four legs
       dancing in anticipation
          eyes glued ...

Lady ...

what was really "Lady"
    was that unconditional love,
        that total trust,
that joy at being remembered,
    acknowledged and patted,
        that look that said:

"I love you ...

I am Joy in a woolly coat
    come to dance into your life
        to make you laugh!"

        Oh, Lady ...
    today I weep,
It is so hard
    to say goodbye.
I'll miss you
    my lady friend.

Lady died today.

I felt release. Three other pets remained in my care. For Perro's sake, particularly, I needed to be there for them. I wondered just what Perro was experiencing. How does a dog feel loss? He did not come out from behind the sofa at all that first night and I sensed his hurt. I never fathomed how much I would hurt. Perro and I expressed mutual empathy. In a characteristic way, he rested his chin on my lap and "talked" to me, sometimes audibly and other times with his soft, penetrating gaze that united our hearts. "You miss Lady, don't you?" I whispered. "I do, too, Perro, I do, too."

REMEMBERING

Life beyond Grief

Dogs—our animal friends—
what a joy!
And they offer that joy,
their gift of life, for us
to share. When they move on
the gift remains.
Let us treasure it.

Perro and Lady

12

Grief: A Process

With Lady's death a new consciousness unfolded. A deepening awareness and reverence for life entered my being. Yet, I endured a searing sense of loss and sorrow as well. I became cognizant once again of what I have always known to be true—the painful experiences in life often provide the opportunity for substantial spiritual growth. Our part lies in recognizing this opportunity and mastering its difficult challenges. If we do this we will emerge triumphant over our pain, and for that we can also thank our animal friends.

For the first time, I realized the pain of losing an animal friend provides just as valid an opportunity for spiritual growth as the loss of a human friend. After all, a beloved pet's death can be just as painful an experience as a human death. Both can elicit an equally intense sense of grief. Too often, however, people respond to the pet owner's grief with insensitivity; their typical response being: "After all, it was only an animal." It is important to recognize the need to provide individual or group support during the very real, normal, and necessary process of grief which accompanies pet loss.

To some, death is an alien experience; to others, it has an altogether too-familiar ring. Whenever death strikes someone close to us, no matter how limited or extensive our experience, we must face a nearly inescapable accompanying pain. Separation, loss, and emptiness deplete our emotions. The very word "strikes" connotes a blow, something to be warded off, a trauma. We seek consolation. We turn to our friends, our counselors, to prayer, to our faith, hoping to comprehend and soften the blow.

Disbelief describes the initial feeling of the griever, a need to deny the loss and pain. Disbelief may actually precede your pet's death. For example, when the suggestion or decision is made to euthanize your pet, you may have to confront a situation that you can't believe has arrived. Given the choice of staying with your pet or not at the time it is euthanized, you may feel you can not bear to stay. If you are not present, you effectually remove yourself from the immediacy of the death; this only heightens your sense of disbelief. When death occurs as a result of an accident, a sudden loss, the disbelief is also accentuated. Called shock, it shields your system from the reality of the unexpected and the pain it evokes. Even expected death presents an abrupt finality. It quite possibly ends a long friendship—a very difficult change to accept. You may withdraw, feeling apathetic or depressed. You may exhibit restless behavior, pacing or wandering aimlessly. You may feel as if you're having a bad dream from which you'll soon awaken. Whatever the reasons for your pet's death, the entire first stage of grief has an air of unreality about it.

When you are ready to move on, a second stage occurs. Reality asserts itself and a storm of emotions may be unleashed. Crying and anger commonly occur. Expressing these feelings to someone who understands —a friend, doctor, or anyone who knew the pet—is therapeutic. When Lady died and I expressed rage, I wanted someone to know and to care. I needed personal contact. I hung up on a telephone answering machine which, of course, couldn't provide instant feedback.

During this stage of grief, you may have a tendency to feel guilt or to blame. "If only" I, or the doctor, or the neighbor, or that dog next door, or God...! I blamed the nameless, faceless public for not grieving with me. Knowing the danger of invoking self-blame, I consciously avoided taking responsibility for not noticing Lady's distress sooner. For some people, bitterness and preoccupation with every aspect of the circumstances surrounding the death compound the guilt and blame. This period can go on for weeks. Be patient. You aren't crazy or too sensitive. Nor do you have misplaced priorities. You feel pain and have every right, indeed healthy need, to express the emotions that come up for you, whatever they may be. Even with my perceptions about death, and Lady's death in particular, the intense pain I felt had to play itself out.

On the afternoon of Lady's death, I returned to the hospital to spend a quiet hour with her body and begin the process of healing. I reminisced and reflected on what she had been to me. I surprised myself somewhat. Contrary to my long-standing plans, I chose not to bring her home for burial. I wanted to feel certain that her spirit had passed on but I no longer felt the need to transport her body home. I couldn't quite bear to leave her soft white fur, however, so I snipped off a memento. A little embarrassed, I stuffed it into my pocket unde-tected by anyone around. That was "my way."

In the next few days, I gathered up all photographs of Lady I could find. I turned my attention to a newly developed roll of film. Among the pictures were several taken just one week before Lady's illness became evi-dent. The dogs and I had gone to the beach that foggy July day and had enjoyed a long walk at the ocean's edge. As the dogs relaxed on the sand I took a number of shots of them against that magnificent backdrop.

Now, as I contemplated the result, a startling photo appeared before my eyes. A subdued Perro dominates the foreground. Lady appears a few paces behind him, ready to take off into the ether, and beyond her a rock outcropping, a silent spector in the fog, awaits her homecoming. The effect was eerie. I drew a sharp breath as the realization dawned: they knew. Did they? Could they? As embodiments of the spirit which exists outside time and space it was entirely possible they knew what was to come. Time and again I came back to that photo with it's beautiful message of infinity—a message which helped me to see endings as a continuity in creation.

Poring over my collection of photos, I participated in the final stage of the grief process—resolution. I moved through my persistent grief, coping with the loss and resolving the many questions surrounding Lady's life, its purpose, my response to her challenge, and the circumstances of her death. Eventually time and a gentle spirit of healing eased the pain, allowing the memories of her life to wash over my consciousness suffused with new feelings of joy and delight.

"Goodby, my friend."

13

Sorrow in a Woolly Coat

My awareness of an animal's perceptions about death began with the photo of Lady and Perro on the beach. This awareness intensified as I heard stories of behavior which clearly indicated that animals experience sadness, grief, and loss as well as an uncanny perception about death.

Sparky, a very cute, playful Cock-a-poo, is a member of a family whose dear son, Dimitri, lost his life in a car accident. Sparky actually "belonged" to the boy's younger brother, Damien, but Dimitri became especially attached to the dog and vice versa. Every day brought the two together in play. Dimitri was popular in school and active in sports. On the day following his tragic accident, many friends and teammates gathered at his home. Together with the family and their parish priest, they formed a circle, joined hands, and recited the Lord's Prayer. At that moment, Sparky came to the center of the healing circle, put back his head, and moaned in a totally uncharacteristic way. The sound he emitted had never been heard before, a very clear sound of grief—and comfort—to all present.

Poupette was a nineteen-year-old Poodle who, at age thirteen, trained the household's newcomer, Suzie, a baby Shih-Tzu. Suzie followed the older dog's example, emulating her as she carried out the day's activities. The two dogs became good friends. After long years of good health, Poupette quite suddenly became ill and within two weeks deteriorated rapidly. Age had caught up with her, swiftly incapacitating her.

Dave, her owner, was away from home on a business trip and therefore not present when the veterinarian humanely advised having Poupette euthanized. Dave's wife knew he would want to see Poupette one more time to say goodbye. Since he was due home the next day, the euthanasia was delayed. Normally, both dogs would have come to the door to enthusiastically greet Dave on his return. This time, however, neither Suzie nor Poupette appeared.

Dave found them on a special mat set down for Poupette, both on their tummies, nose to nose, transferring information. Neither Dave nor anything else could break their concentration. "It's up to you now, Suzie. Goodbye, my friend," Poupette seemed to be saying. Following the death of her mentor, Suzie carried on exactly as she had been "taught," with love and devotion.

Two Bits, a miniature Schnauzer of sorts, responded to death with feelings we tend to call "human." Although Two Bits belonged to Hazel, my friend and customer, he showed a great fondness for her father. This mutual feeling grew stronger when the man came to live with Hazel following his wife's death. Hazel worked during the day, leaving the man and dog to spend many hours in each others' exclusive company. They became close companions.

When Hazel's father died, Two Bits appeared to be in mourning. He sat for hours at the closed door of the man's room, waiting for his friend to come out. He reverted to his pre-house-training manners and generally misbehaved. An acquaintance of Hazel's suggested she purchase a cat to be a companion for Two Bits, to turn his attention from his loss. The plan worked. The dog attached himself to the kitten and today, some nine years later, the two are inseparable. Two Bits had never been one to want handling or cuddling but he did need companionship. He seemed to pour out his love and grief and sense of caring to another living being. It was as if he needed to be needed to assuage his grief.

Rascal Ragmop and Sammy Cat

14

Joy Wears Another Coat

Nose to nose, heart to heart, we creatures of
earth do bond to one another. Although my
attention has always been drawn towards dogs,
our household often included a cat or two. During my
teaching days, to the pleasure of the school children,
both guinea pigs and a rabbit became members of the
classroom, providing a wonderful learning opportunity.
Respect, compassion, and responsibility went hand in
hand with the fun of animal companionship. The stu-
dents took turns taking the pets into their homes for
weekend care and endured the illness and death of our
mother guinea pig. We all grieved and helped one
another deal with the sadness.

Although my experiences with dogs passing away
might have suggested the extent to which bonding can
take place with all kinds of animals, my more recent
work with grief support has strongly impressed me with
the depth of this bond in any human-animal relationship. Through my work, I have come to know better the

particularly heartfelt connection experienced by the wonderful breed of people known as "cat lovers." They number in the millions. Through them my appreciation has grown for the singular creatures they adore.

Cat lovers use a common vernacular to describe their feline friends: independent, inscrutable, and aloof. However, intense loyalty, heightened affection, and undeniable intelligence also categorize these special four-footed friends. Their almost-dual nature—the wild and the domestic—sets cats apart and most certainly differentiates them from their very domesticated counterpart, the dog.

I often hear about unusual cats; indeed, cats considered not only unusual but unique in the eyes of their owners. Dog lovers rarely use that term in describing their canine friends. Practically any dog can easily learn to sit, shake hands, or roll over on command. Their obedience is common enough to be unremarkable. When a cat obeys commands, however (and nearly every cat owner I have encountered has a cat who does some sort of trick), cat owners and observers alike are thrilled at this responsiveness in such a reputedly aloof creature. A bond *does* exist between cat lovers and their pets that is every bit as deep, loving, and communicative as the bond between dogs and their owners.

Cat lovers may also be dealing with a bond established over a much longer period of time than most dogs will ever live. It is not unusual for a cat to live as long as twenty years! The current of love and devotion can run very deep during such a long friendship. This is underscored by the amazing, poignant, and delightful stories cat lovers who have lost their pets recount as they shed their tears and try to come to some sense of comfort, if not understanding, surrounding their loss.

I have heard it said that cats are "very spiritual." My own experience with this quality has been with Sammy Cat—as affectionate yet unassuming a fellow as you'll ever see. When I take time to quiet my thoughts and relax in a somewhat meditative state, Sammy Cat will invariably place his large feline body right over my heart as if mesmerized by the stillness. Is this truly spiritual attunement? Perhaps. I've noticed and wondered.

Cats frequently bond with other creatures of the animal world. In my own family I have witnessed a remarkable affinity between Sammy Cat and his immediate "siblings," as well as the many foreign faces which cross our doorstep. In his own quiet way he checks out the visitors and politely gets across his message—he'll take no guff from anyone. No true disagreements have ever broken out.

A particularly engaging friendship has developed between Sammy and the newest member of my family, Rascal Ragmop. This wonderful woolly delight adopted me on Mother's Day, 1986, and has become a special addition to the fold. Fortune smiled on us all that day in May.

Rounding a bend in the road as I left a family gathering, I spied a black form slithering along on its belly. I was directly in front of the home of Roscoe, a much-loved little black dog I had groomed many times. I wondered how he had gotten out and whether his owners knew. I stopped and called to him by name. The "form" scurried over to my car door.

"Why you rascal," I exclaimed. "You're not Roscoe,

are you?" The form answered by wiggling up onto my lap. Patter, patter went a long, matted plume at one end of its body. I turned the car around and started back the way I had come, looking for a pursuing owner.

I encountered a woman who explained that yes, she was looking for the little dog because it had been wandering up and down the road all day, apparently lost. With nightfall approaching she was worried about its safety. She expressed profound relief when I offered to take the little one home, clean her up, and advertise a "found" dog. I turned the car around once more and set off for home with this dirty little rag-a-muffin by my side. The next day I posted signs and placed ads in the newspapers. Two weeks went by. No calls came in and the signs faded without soliciting one response.

I really questioned the universe for sending still another creature to our already-full family. No such doubts crossed Rascal Ragmop's mind, however. She had come to stay. She showed classic signs of previous abuse —cowering, trembling, hesitation, and fear of the word "come." I worked slowly and gently with her, aided by a tolerant and loving Sammy Cat. He intrigued Rascal and she attracted and challenged him. She was only six months old, yet she rapidly learned "cat" was an integral, fascinating part of her world.

Actually, Rascal herself exhibited cat-like behavior as part of her personality. Warm, sunny days found her perched on the railing outdoors, swatting flying insects with her paw. She and Sammy spent playtime engaged in pursuing each other's tails. Their friendship grew and today includes playful chase-and-be-chased interaction and even sleeping together on occasion.

As time went by, Rascal's appearance changed dramatically. Her form filled out and she now displays a beautiful, shiny, black, flowing coat—at least when she sits still long enough for a comb-out! A breeder of Tibetan Terriers tells me that is exactly what I have acquired. Rascal's infectious personality captures the hearts of all who meet her. Sweetness itself, she displays a totally engaging rapture towards her life and those of us privileged to make up her world. I thank the spirit of the universe for this precious package of love.

Love: Yours for the Asking

15

New Friends

When our pets die, many considerations surround our individual and personal decisions to find another. Coupled with the fears of not being able to face the eventual pain of pet loss may be the question of ever being able to love another animal as much as we loved our departed friend. Indeed, there may be a sense of guilt surrounding the issues of love and loyalty.

It seems to me that if we have loved another living being to such a degree that we grieve so deeply, we are capable of a great deal of love. And love by its very nature reaches out and expands. Love cannot be stored away. To try to do so clogs the corridors of our emotional being. On the other hand, one person's love, freely given, opens that person's entire being and in the process contributes to the consciousness of the whole universe.

We can never "replace" a beloved companion, yet we can choose to fill the void with new life and love. Many people need time to work through their grieving before beginning the experience of raising and loving a pet again. For me this was not an issue. Lady left behind several of her friends, so no sense of urgency pushed me to look for another dog. Some people look forward to more flexibility in their lives and choose to postpone the responsibility and care of another pet. Others feel an immediate desire to share in the life and love of an animal again.

In her touching tribute to Patches,[2] Jane Hutchison closes with these words: "Eventually we will take another...dog into our home. No dog can ever replace Patches, but sharing with another dog the love she left us seems the only fitting way to honor her memory. Although Patches is gone, her spirit, her memory, and her love will always remain with us." Whenever we're ready, the right companion eagerly awaits adoption. Endearing, amazing, entertaining, energetic, reserved, or something in between—each new animal offers a unique package of love and joy.

One of my dear, elderly customers, Rose, lost her home companion of thirteen years. When her departed dog, Mollie, was alive I heard Rose exclaim over and over, "Why this little Mollie-Gal means more to me than anything else in my life! She's the reason I get up some mornings." Mollie's death meant more to Rose than losing her friend, it meant losing her very purpose in life! She mourned her friend and felt having a new little dog to love would be the only way to recover from her loss. Her own failing health concerned her.

---

[2]This tribute, entitled *Only the Love Remains*, was published in the Santa Clara County Humane Society newsletter. It is Ms. Hutchison's heart-wrenching commentary on the life and death of her beloved dog Patches.

"Is it fair," Rose asked me, "to take in a new dog when I might not live as long as it will?"

Rose wanted and needed a new friend, a new purpose in life. Many in her position want a home companion but fear starting over. Making advance preparation for competent and loving care of your pet in case of illness or even death can ease that fear. If you do not have a trusted friend or family member whom you can call on, your veterinarian can help you choose an appropriate person. There are a number of service groups all over the country that provide such help.

Of course the name of the person or group you wish to rely on must be left where it will be found. Choose an obvious place in your house to display that information, and be sure to leave it with your veterinarian, as well. Ensure your pet's welfare and your peace of mind, and follow your desire to find a new friend. Don't deprive either yourself or the lucky newcomer!

A few months ago, Rose proudly introduced me to her new puppy, a gift from her daughter. She was thrilled! Clearly visible on her refrigerator door are emergency instructions to be followed should she become incapacitated, and Muffin heads the list. Rose still sheds a tear for Mollie and still tells me that no other pet could ever be the same. (How true!) However, with pride and joy she calls after me now as I carry the puppy out the door to be groomed, "Take good care of my Muffin. I don't know what I'd do without her. You know, she's the light of my life!"

Rose's experience is not unique. Many wonderful stories can be told about the positive role home companions play in the lives of the elderly. I enjoy a special friendship with Marianne, age seventy-eight, which has continued since my early grooming days. Fluffy, her adorable white-and-gray Cock-a-poo, not only brought us together but can take full credit for providing a healthy, enriching routine in Marianne's life. From daily walks around the neighborhood, with Fluffy literally prancing into the hearts of all they meet, to those special moments of relating quietly to another being who cares, Fluffy and Marianne fill each other's needs.

A recent trip east occasioned a chance conversation aboard an airliner. "I don't know what I would have done without my little dog," began a lovely white-haired lady. "When I had to put my husband in a nursing home, she was such a comfort to me. Oh, how she filled the void! When she died I grieved so. I have a cat now. I wasn't sure but he's very sweet. Cats are very mysterious, you know!" These words were accompanied by a range of emotions—the pain of remembering a husband's last journey, the joy and then sadness over her little dog-friend, and then, with a twinkle in her eye, delight at this mysterious new companion in her life.

Perro

16

Spirit in the Flesh

Spirit works through all forms of life as an energy force. Anyone closely associated with animals knows what a highly developed sensory awareness of energy flow they exhibit. Let an unsavory character approach an animal and watch the animal pick up on the person instantly. Let an animal lover approach and see how attuned the animal becomes to that energy vibration. Animals sense changes in the forces of nature, sometimes days before the change manifests. (In China animal behavior is a respected harbinger of coming earthquakes.) And when an animal is sick, it tends to withdraw, to go into the silence—to another place in its consciousness—communing, perhaps, with the spirit within.

I agree with those who feel the above reactions have a purely rational basis. Animals do respond differently to vibrations than do human beings, their sense of smell or hearing is more highly developed, and when they are sick they innately know to be quiet in order to facilitate healing. I also suggest that behind, or beyond, or within each of these reactions dwells the powerful life force, which I call Spirit, working through each animal according to its form.

A few weeks after Lady's death, I felt that Spirit move through Perro. Together, he and I experienced a powerful energy exchange that truly humbled me and opened wide my appreciation of the interplay of Spirit between human and animal.

Eight years earlier, Perro had suffered his first epileptic seizure. Away from home at the time, I received a phone call telling me Perro had been poisoned and asking me to please come home. I froze, so frightened of Perro's dying that I became immobile. As I was being driven home, my veterinarian friend came to the house. He diagnosed epilepsy, not poisoning. By the time I arrived home Perro had come out of his seizure and was nearly back to normal, to my overwhelming relief. The doctor explained what had happened and described seizures, their symptoms, and the procedure for dealing with them.

Over the next several years, Perro's seizures took place cyclically, every six months. A couple of days prior to an attack, he exhibited strange, needy behavior. Leaning and brushing against me, he commanded my complete attention. As the seizure took hold, he began to salivate profusely and lose control of his limbs. His eyes glazed over as I held his feverish head and tried to soothe him. Every attack frightened and confused him. My presence seemed to reassure him and reduce the stress.

In September, 1985, Perro again experienced his regular six-month seizure. In November, two more took place only ten days apart. Until then, because of the infrequency of the attacks, no medicine had been prescribed. However, with this change in pattern, my veterinarian friend thought it appropriate to begin medication.

It took some time and experimentation to find the appropriate medicine and regulate the dosage. Before enough time had passed to complete that process, Perro showed all the signs of another seizure, affording me an excellent opportunity to work with him, utilizing my increasing awareness of the movement of Spirit through life's many forms.

Summoning my own inner source of strength and love and healing, I held Perro as I always do. But this time I consciously allowed the energy flow—the spirit of life and healing—to flow through me. I asked that this life force go through Perro, dissolving anything not of itself. The dog looked at me curiously and began to relax. His taut limbs resumed their normal position and he sighed in contentment. He continued to watch me and I petted him awhile longer. Then he came to his feet, completely normal in appearance and manner.

Never before had I experienced anything like that! What actually took place? I'm not sure. I felt that a wondrous and beautiful Universal Spirit had flowed between us.

17

"...Elegant, dignified,
kind, noble dog-person!
We'll all miss you...."

With these words my dear friend and veterinarian Dieter laid Perro to rest. It was a lovely Sunday morning in September, 1987, two weeks to the day after Perro had refused his morning meal—unusual behavior I attributed to his solo romp around the neighborhood the previous Saturday night. "You turkey," I admonished him. "Stuck your nose in someone's garbage, did you? Well, no matter. Your breakfast will keep until you're hungry." Indeed, later the same day he consumed most of the food. Monday morning, however, brought another refusal and he lacked his usual exuberance on our daily walk in nearby Redwood Regional Park.

Three weeks earlier Perro had been operated on for removal of a large lipoma (fatty tissue tumor). He had recovered quickly and completely. On this Monday I stopped by the veterinary hospital for flea treatment products.

"How's Perro?" the doctor asked.

"Fine," I replied, thinking of his remarkable recovery. On reflection I added, "Well, actually he does not seem to be feeling well. He isn't eating."

"Does he seem depressed"? asked my friend. To my affirmative reply he suggested I bring Perro in for a check-up fairly soon. At home I took Perro's temperature—104 degrees—two degrees above normal.

"First thing tomorrow," I told Perro, "we'll get you fixed up." In his characteristic way he gazed up at me and uttered soft, moaning "communications" which I understood to be his total trust, acceptance, and patience. Then he stretched out to rest until morning. Little did I realize then that come morning we would be embarking on the last series of "trips to the vet" we would be making together.

No evidence of Perro's usual perky pleasure accompanied the next day's visit to the hospital. Being a nervous mother, I could not bear to see him so low in spirits. His silent plea for help moved my very being. It did not take long for Dieter to discover that some part of Perro's abdominal region was experiencing acute distress. An x-ray was ordered. I would need to leave him there until later in the day. "Call at four o'clock," Dieter advised.

And so began a long, stressful week of medical treatment—the x-rays, exploratory surgery, biopsies, blood work-ups, a blood transfusion, a night in emergency with a 105.4 degree temperature and then finally a second and last transfusion, using the healthy, rich blood of a black Labrador neighbor, Yuki. Yuki's generous, compassionate owners knew the depth of my anxiety and wanted to help in some way. I feel especially grateful to them. Had Perro not received Yuki's blood he could not have come home, a homecoming important to both of us. We needed to be together for his last days.

One week after our initial visit, my gallant Perro walked out of the hospital under his own power. With a boost from me he settled himself on a Mexican blanket in the back of my car and came home for the final time. It was Tuesday, September 1, 1987.

That previous week had been a nightmare for me. All veterinary personnel held out hope for Perro's recovery—for a turnaround. And yet as I stood by him during his ordeal I felt certain I was watching my dog die. Everything known was being done for Perro and yet I felt helpless. His immune system was not functioning properly. He was destroying his red blood cells, storing this debris in his liver, and steadily weakening from the resulting anemia.

I'd have done anything to heal him. Once he came home I think I knew in my soul that he *was* being healed—only his healing would come in the form of death. Yet, out of this nightmare a beauty began to emerge. I found myself praying aloud, "Thank you for this blessing," and knowing in some ineffable way that it *was* a blessing. I ached for Perro and in the ache recognized the most powerful feeling of love I have ever known. I loved another being totally and the depth of my feeling sobered me. I recognized the special blessing and, once again, the opportunity this experience provided me. I knew Perro's time had come and together, with God showing us how, we would get through whatever the next hours or days brought. We "talked," I cried, we simply sat together, his head resting in my lap. The air of unreality experienced with Lady enveloped me. Time stood still. We waited.

Particularly touching to me was the outpouring of support Perro and I experienced—friends and neighbors stopping by, letters and phone calls of inquiry and comfort, a card addressed to "Sr. Perro Church," and Dieter's daily visit. One of Perro's favorite "people-friends" was Tom, who had been our upstairs neighbor for three years, renting that part of the house. Tom came by every day to be with Perro, to share secrets with him. Although his body was very weak, Perro always acknowledged his friend.

Perro's illness and approaching death became a wonderful opportunity for the children who knew him. Marty and Willie, who had played with him, walked him, and fed him many times when I had to be away, visited him together with their mother. Andy and Sarah, who were learning for the first time about caring for a sick animal, came to see him, to pat him, to talk to him. They had known him as a large, strong, lovable friend and now they had been told he was dying. They asked the frank, innocent questions so typical of children: "Is he sick? Can he play? You're going to feel sad when he dies, aren't you?" They learned and practiced compassion.

"You could ask God to bless him," said four-year-old Andy.

"I do, Andy, all the time," I responded.

"I do, too," this sweet little boy replied.

When Perro grew weaker Marty and Willie came to help dig Perro's grave, along with their mother and Andy and Sarah's parents. I assisted in this process and to my surprise found it to be therapeutic. I needed to know that a spot in the earth was prepared to receive this proud, dignified dog I loved so much. Aloud I wondered what I might place near his grave as a marker.

"You could take some clay and mold his paw in it," suggested five-year-old Willie. "That way he'll always be with us." Remarkable wisdom from the heart of one so young.

Another friend, Norma (we met many years earlier through her dog, FSBO), brought the clay and we did mold Perro's paw, with only the mildest of protests from him. I told him it was for a good cause. Wise old soul, he probably knew. Norma came by often. One day she brought him a special broth she had made from scratch. It remained untouched—at least by Perro. The little dogs appreciated its tasty addition to their evening meals. Most important, Norma brought her love which I know Perro felt. It was very difficult for her to let him go. I'm glad she had the opportunity to say goodbye and I'm enormously grateful to her for the tender support she gave to both of us.

The last full day of Perro's life was Saturday, September 5. After what had seemed to be a rally the day before, his condition noticeably changed. He showed great weakness and lacked the apparent desire to raise his head as I came and went. Prior to Saturday he had showed total awareness of where I was at all times. He always raised himself to a half-prone position where he could visually observe what was going on. Once when I gave in to my tears he continued to reach for me, to place his soft muzzle against my wet cheek. Those gentle wise eyes followed my every move. Dieter had assured me that Perro was in no pain. He had prepared me for Saturday's weakened condition, saying this weakness would progress until Perro's heart stopped. Death would not be dramatic in its actuality.

The sadness of the vigil I had kept the past twelve days culminated Saturday. I did not think I could take much more. Tom stopped by again.

"Does Perro know that its okay for him to go?" he asked. "Have you told him?" I wasn't sure. Had I thought only of myself?

When Tom left I knelt by Perro's side and took his face in my hands. "I'll be just fine, Perro," I told him. "You must not worry. I'll miss you very much but I'll be fine. And Perro, I'll *always* love you." At those words Perro laid his head back upon the blanket. He never again raised it.

I did not want to leave Perro and I also did not want to hear his last breath. I prayed. At 3:25 a.m. as I listened to his shallow breathing I thought, I can't do this. I put my soft feather pillow over my ears and turned over to try to sleep. At that very instant I knew. I removed the pillow and the room was still—still and *peaceful*.

An enormous sense of release enveloped me. I went over to Perro and told him, as I had hundreds of times over his twelve-and-a-half years, that he was perfect. He had done well and his own release was richly deserved. I covered him with a blanket and then, going to my own bed, I slept a deep much-needed sleep.

The next morning I called Dieter to tell him and ask if he wished to participate in Perro's burial. He'd said he'd be by at ten o'clock. I spread the word to others who would want to know. Norma came by one last time. At a little before ten, Dieter and Andy and Sarah's father arrived. With utter affection they carried Perro to his resting place. The sole observer of our rites, Sammy Cat, watched from a nearby deck. Whatever he thought or felt he kept to himself.

> "...Elegant, dignified,
> kind, noble dog-person!
> We'll all miss you...."

In Tribute

September 6, 1987

With dignity and gentleness of heart,
   my uncommon friend
      completed his mission as he saw it.
He came in love, he left in love,
   slipping out so softly one could but imagine
      a gentle breeze, nothing more.
Behind he leaves a mighty wind,
   an expression of unconditional love,
      a power to heal the planet earth.

For this beloved friend *was* love.
   Total,
      joyous,
         unconditional love.
Through his eyes one sensed
   Truth,
      wisdom,
         compassion.

Only a dog?
   The most treasured of values,
      the most tender of passions, my Perro.

May he run forever
   on the beaches and trails
      of the kingdom beyond.

Woo-ah woo-ooo-ooo!

He greets the morning,
   head held high, eyes sparkling,
      calling the troops to a day of adventure.
Fleet beauty,
   a dance of joy,
      sharing time with so many stories to tell.
And then to close the day,
   a quiet lift of his head,
      from his favorite resting spot at bedside.
With dignity and gentleness of heart,
   my uncommon friend
      said good night.

Good night, my Perro, God bless you.

Epilogue

A steady companion escorted my ongoing journey with my dogs. The same Spirit of the universe I felt with Perro accompanied me, expressing its wondrous energy through each of my animal friends. The various personalities of these creatures played their individual parts in unfolding the lessons of the spirit: compassion, helping me learn to let go, to discover new and deep levels of communication, to appreciate the beauty of now, and to love unconditionally. Perhaps above all, I learned respect for the animals themselves. To know them is to want to know more about them—their inner world and their unique contribution to all the world. In a sense my journey is just beginning!

The provocative words of Dostoevsky's Father Zossima in *The Brothers Karamazov* provide guidance to all of us who wish to expand our understanding and knowledge. He directs us to:

> Love all God's creation.... Love the animals, love the plants, love everything. If you love everything, you will perceive the divine mystery in things. And once you have perceived it, you will begin to comprehend it

more and more every day. And you will come at last to love the whole world with an all-embracing love. Love the animals: God has given them the rudiments of thought and untroubled joy. Do not, therefore, trouble it, do not harass them, do not deprive them of their joy, do not go against God's intent.... Man, do not exalt yourself above the animals: they are without sin.

Dogs—our animal friends—what a joy! And they offer that joy, their gift of life, for us to share. When they move on, the gift remains. Let us treasure it.

About the Author
and Illustrator

Julie Adams Church, a native of Madison, Wisconsin, resides in the Montclair hills of Oakland, California with her three beloved dogs and their friend, Sammy Cat. Animals, people, travel, the ocean and music weave their way through Ms. Church's enthusiastic embrace of life. Her compassionate, outgoing nature has drawn her to teaching elementary school children and later, to establishing and operating her own canine "spa", sharing with others her extraordinary affinity with and understanding of animals. Ms. Church holds a B.S. from the University of Wisconsin-Madison and a MEd. from Xavier University, Cincinnati, Ohio. *Joy in a Woolly Coat* is her first book.

Constance Coleman is widely acknowledged as one of the foremost animal portraitists of our time. She has developed an unparalleled understanding of the domestic animal in all its varieties and personalities. Her individually commissioned paintings attest to her outstanding technique and uncompromising dedication to capturing the spirit as well as the form of her subjects. Trained at the California School of Fine Arts under the tutelage of Mark Rothko and David Park, and at

Chouinard Art School in Los Angeles, Ms. Coleman's work is to be found throughout the United States, Canada, and Great Britain.

Books that Transform Lives

Way of the Peaceful Warrior
By Dan Millman

"It may even change the lives of many . . . who peruse its pages." Dr. Stanley Krippner

Opening to Channel: How to Connect with Your Guide
by Sanaya Roman and Duane Packer, Ph.D.

This breakthrough book is the first step-by-step guide to the art of channeling!

Talking with Nature
by Michael J. Roads

"From Australia comes a major new writer, a startling courageous innocent bringing a gift of power and understanding for those reaching toward the inner real." Richard Bach

Creating Money
by Sanaya Roman and Duane Packer, Ph.D.

The bestselling authors of *Opening to Channel* offer the reader the keys to abundance.

Seeds of Light
by Peter Rengel

"Simple is powerful. Peter Rengel has penned universal principles about the core of our lives in clear, often lyrical, prose." Dan Millman

H J Kramer Inc

Books that Transform Lives

The Earth Life Series
by Sanaya Roman, Channel for Orin

Living with Joy, Book I
"I like this book because it describes the way I feel about so many things." Virginia Satir

Personal Power
through Awareness, Book II
"Every sentence contains a pearl . . . " Lilias Folan

H J Kramer Inc